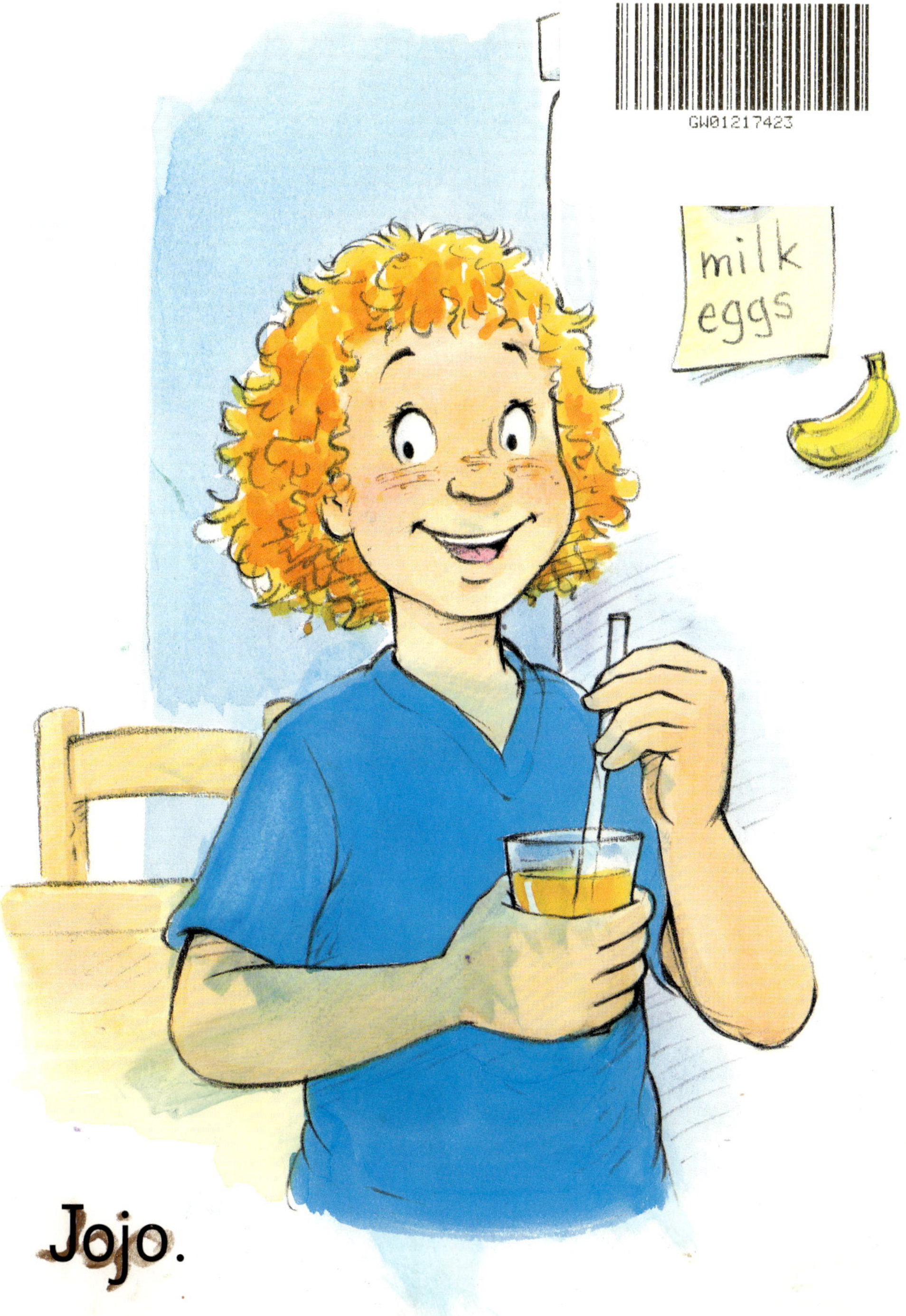

Jojo.

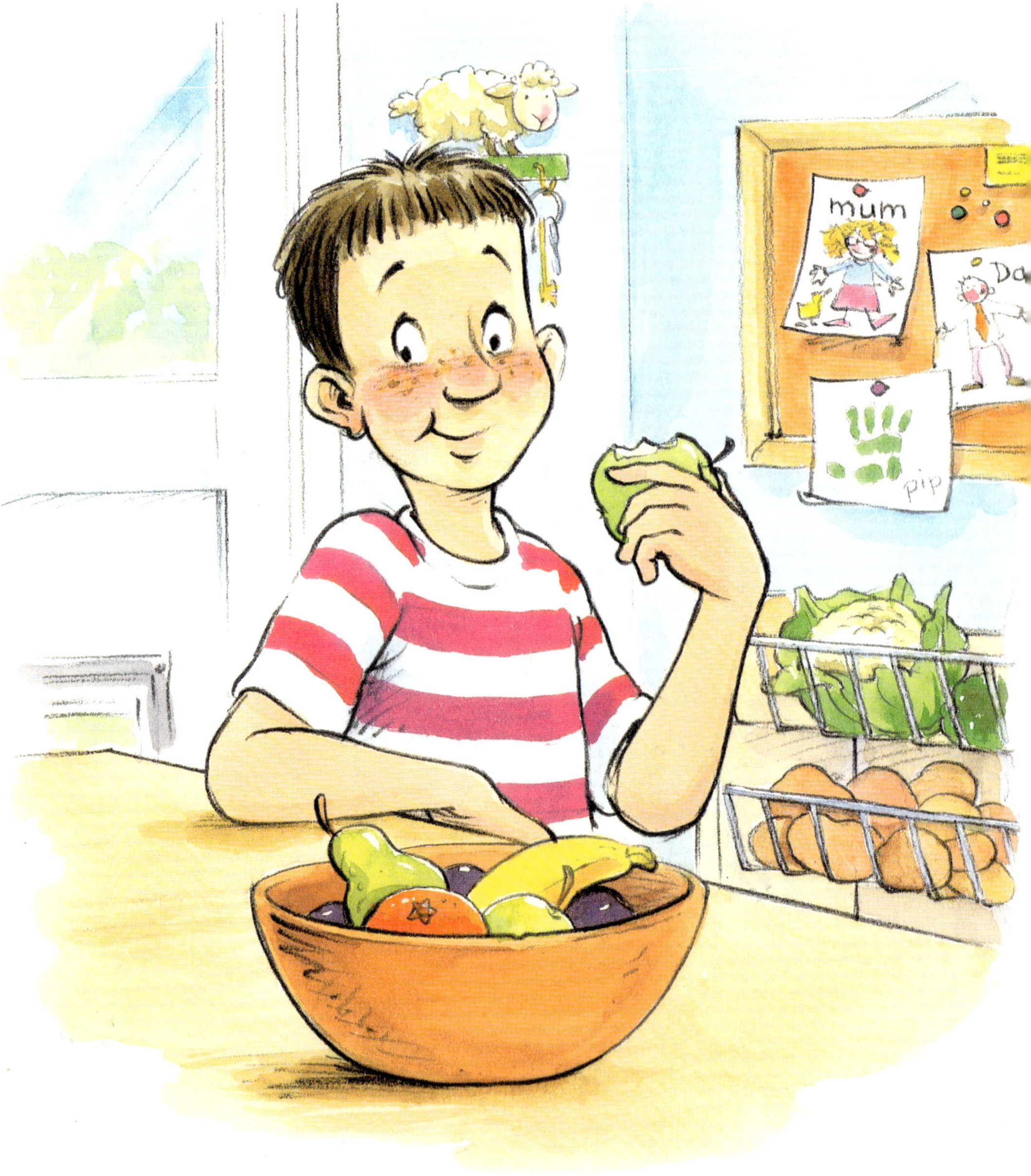

Mouse.

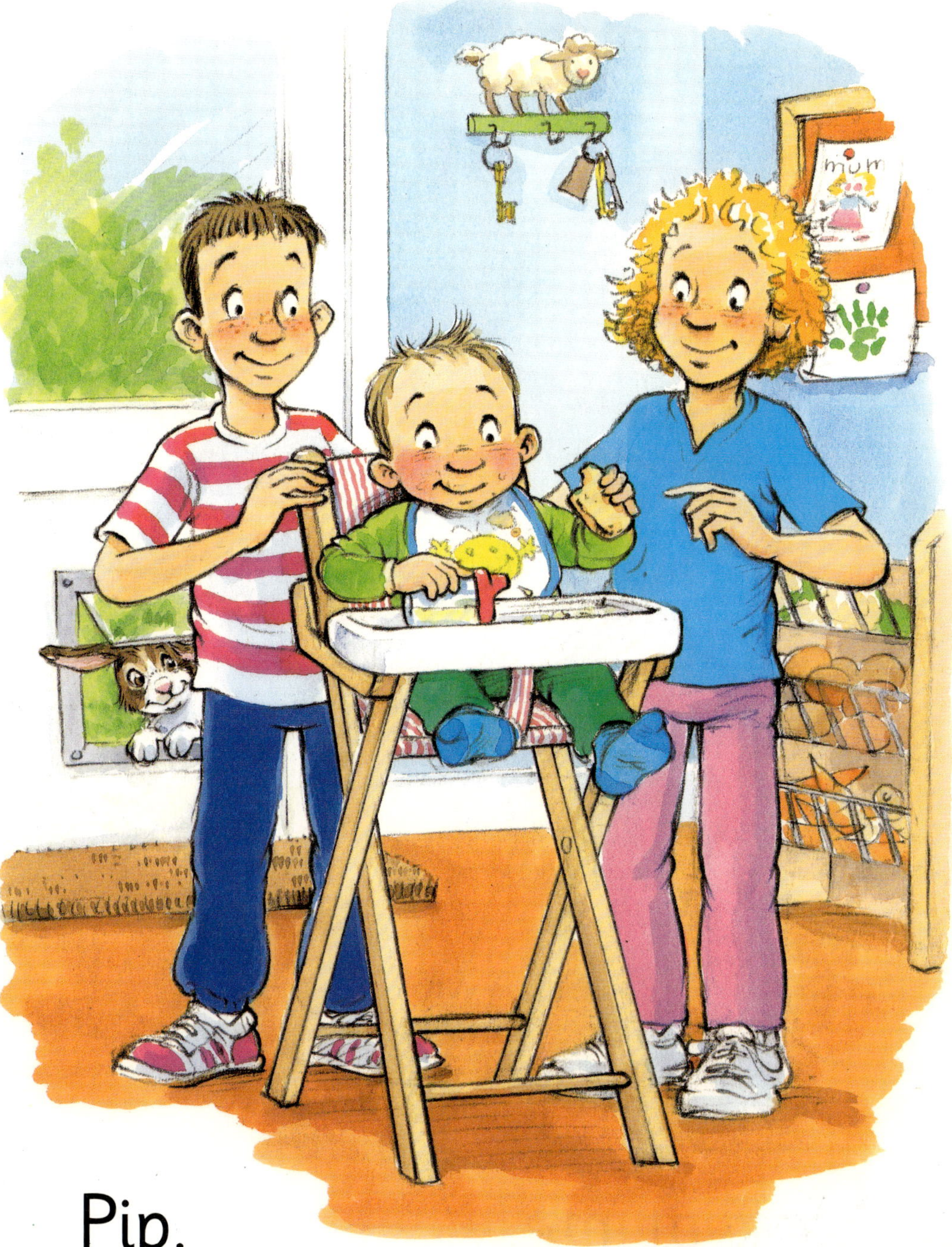

Pip.

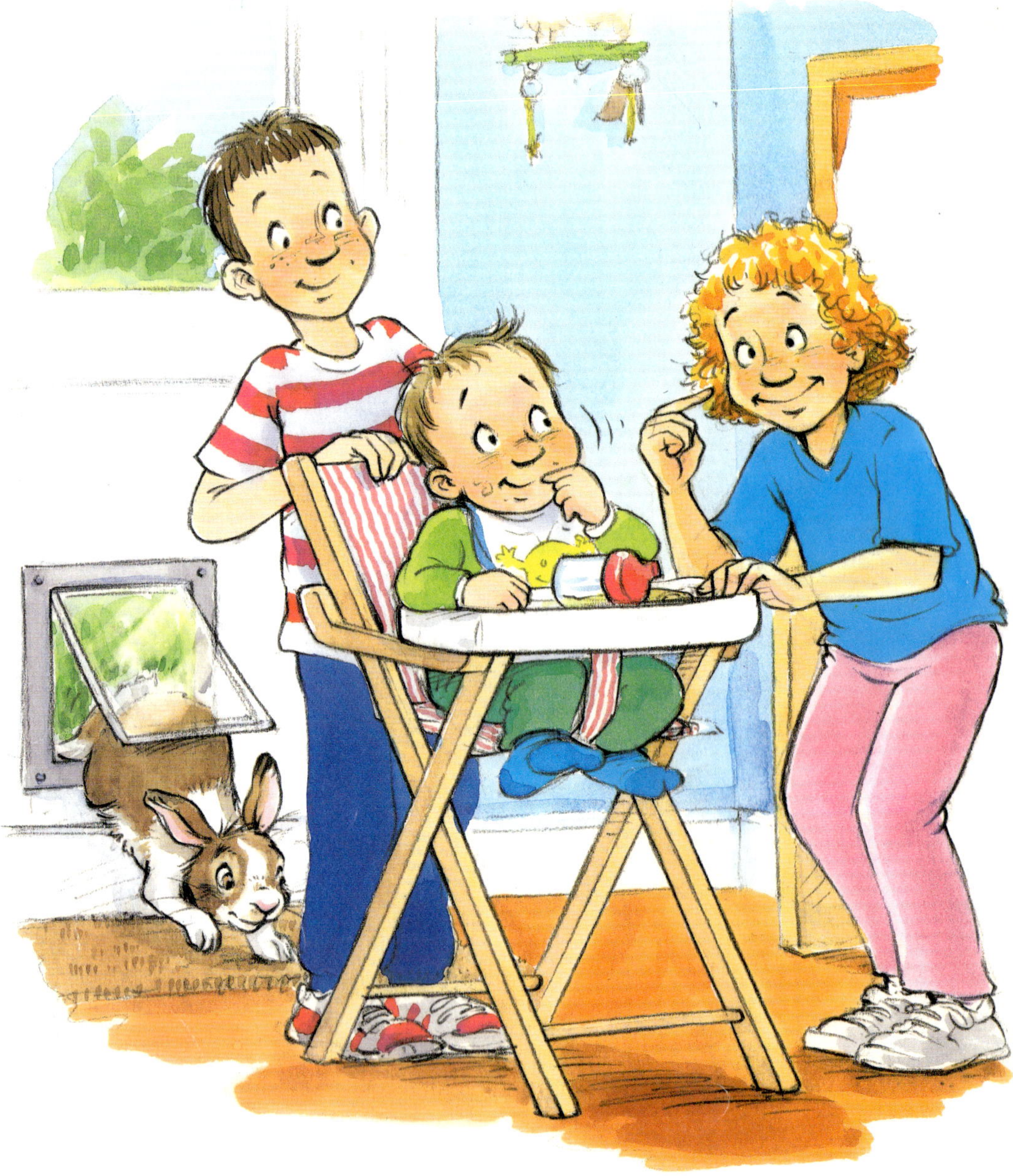

Look at me.

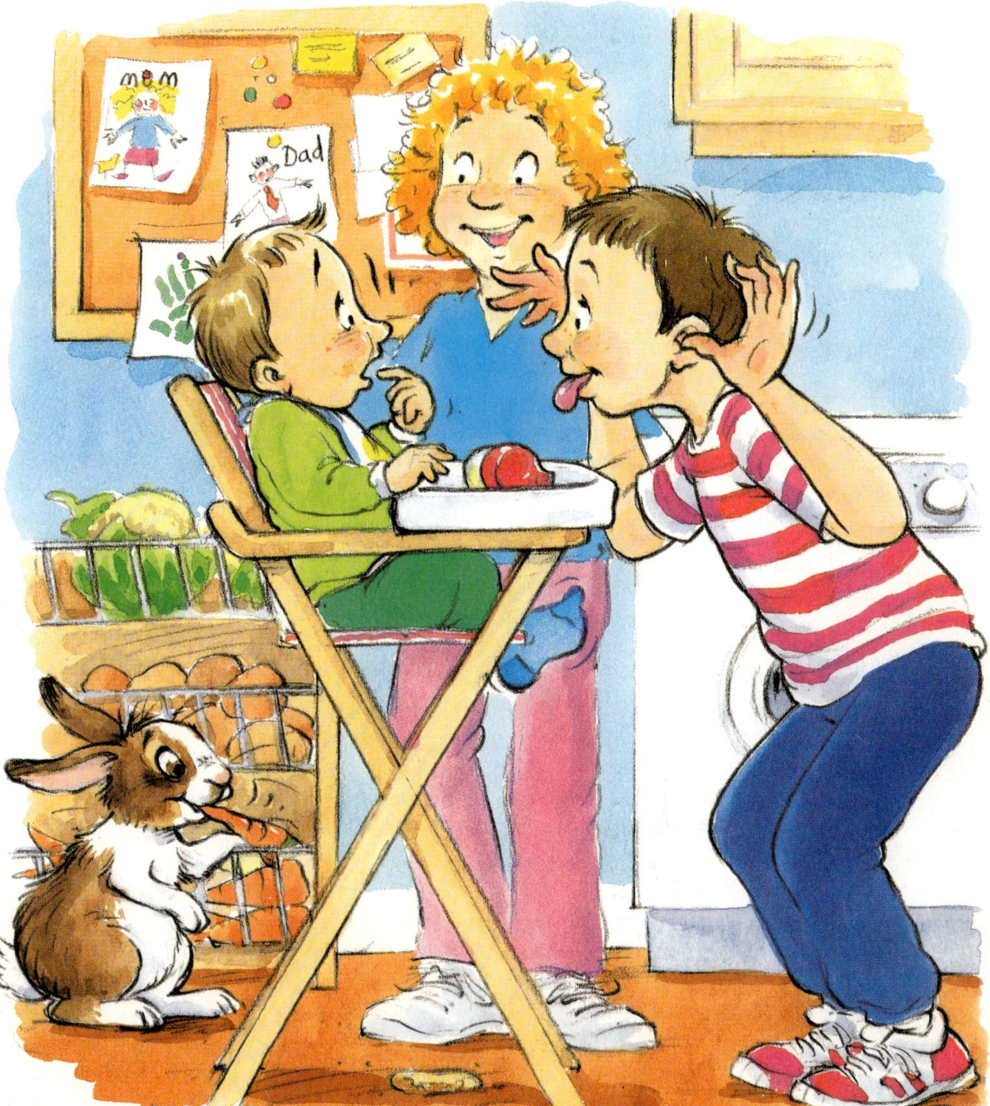

Look at me.

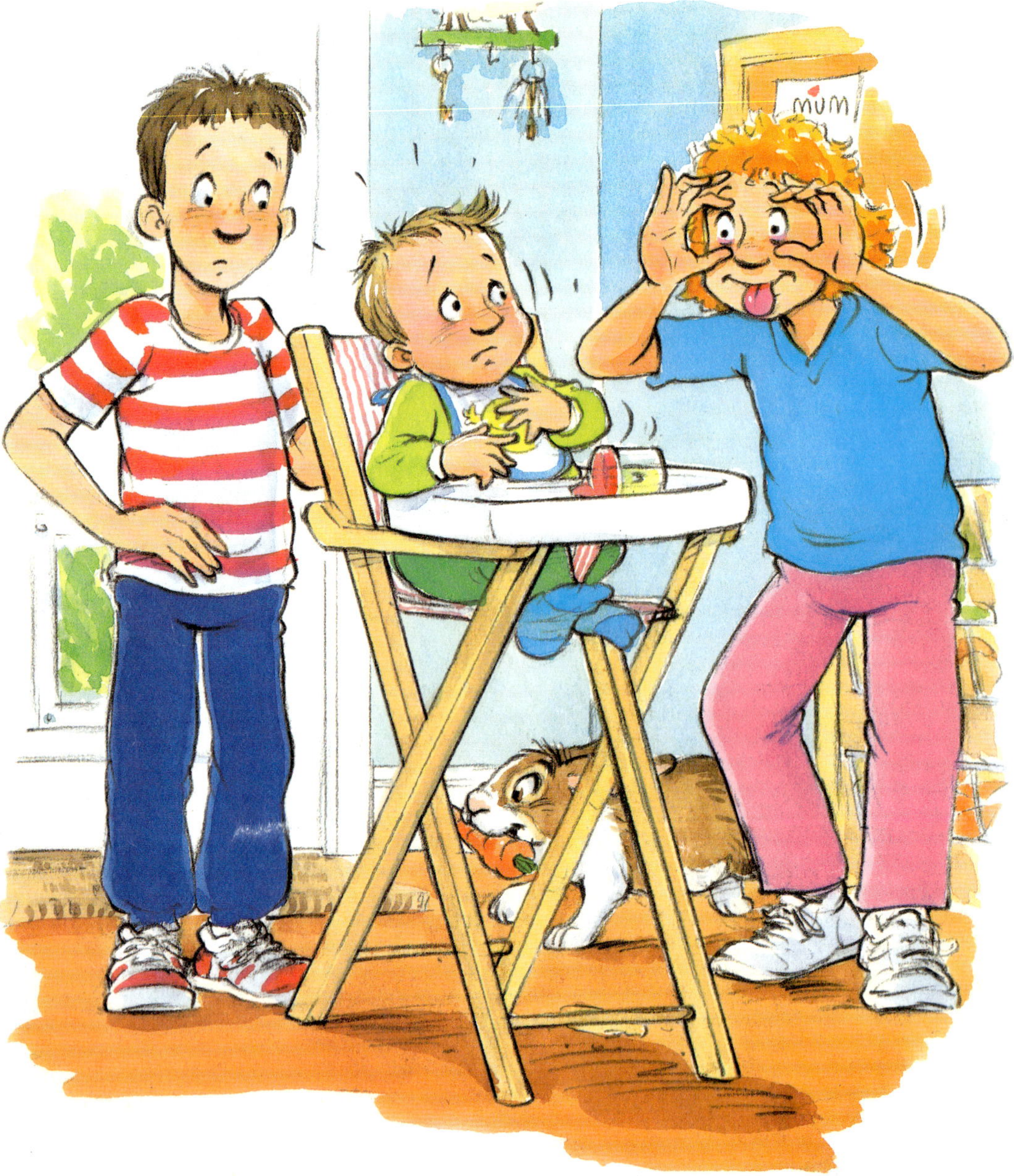

Look at me!

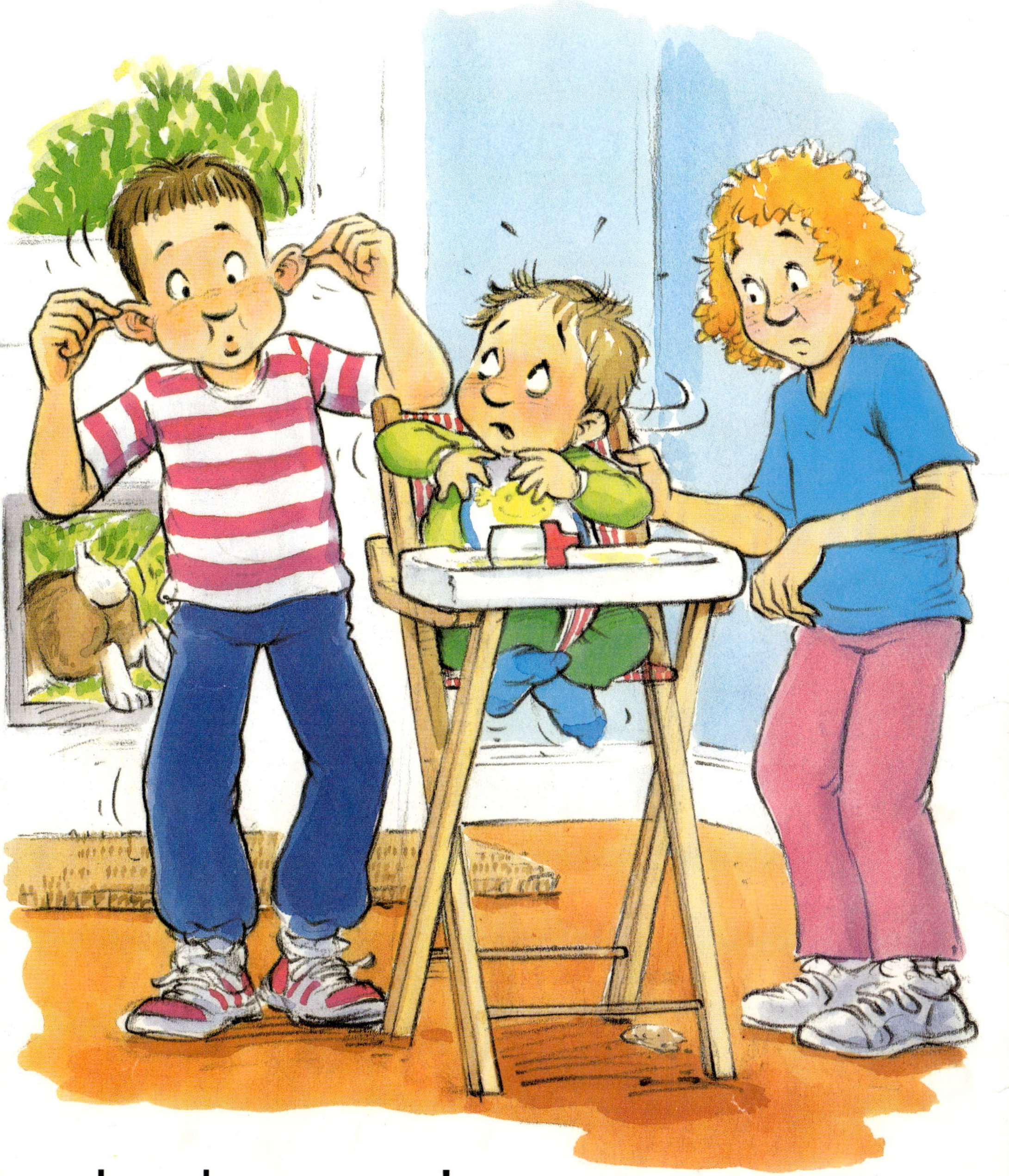

Look at me!

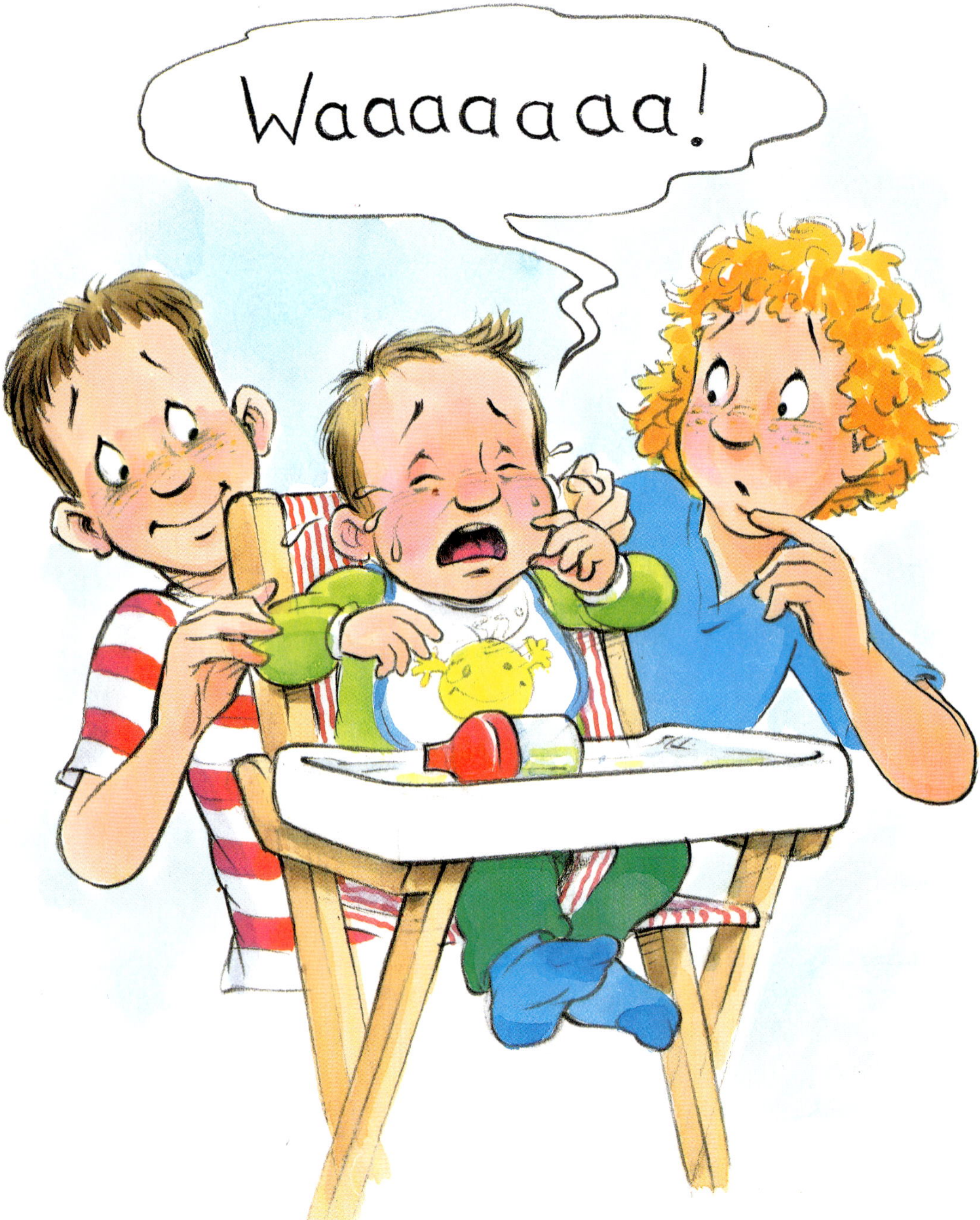
Waaaaaaa!